TOP 10

PARENTS·KEEP OUT!

Pets

A FIREFLY BOOK

Published by Firefly Books Ltd. 2015

Copyright © 2015 Octopus Publishing Group Ltd

First printing

Publisher Cataloging-in-Publication Data (U.S.)

A CIP record for this title is available from the Library of Congress

Library and Archives Canada Cataloguing in Publication

A CIP record for this title is available from Library and Archives Canada

Published in the United States by
Firefly Books (U.S.) Inc.
P.O. Box 1338, Ellicott Station
Buffalo, New York 14205

Published in Canada by
Firefly Books Ltd.
50 Staples Avenue, Unit 1
Richmond Hill, Ontario L4B 0A7

Printed in China

First published in Great Britain in 2015 by Ticktock,
an imprint of Octopus Publishing Group Ltd
Endeavour House
189 Shaftesbury Avenue
London,
WC2H 8JY
Commissioning Editor: Anna Bowles
Senior Production Manager: Peter Hunt

TOP 10

PARENTS KEEP OUT!

Pets

Paul Terry

FIREFLY BOOKS

TOP 10

PARENTS KEEP OUT!

Pets

Team T-10 have explored the world of pets in ways that you would never have imagined possible. Of course we've got plenty of cats and dogs in here, but there are also exotic animals that you would never have guessed would be anyone's pet! The cuddliest creatures on Earth have been given a home, plus there's even a zone dedicated to famous movie and cartoon pets. Brace yourself for a major cute overload...

CONTENTS

MEET...
TEAM T-10

Before you dive into this fact-packed adventure, say hello to the super team ready to guide you through the amazing info zones...

MAY-TRIX

T-10 FILE

This technology-loving 10-year-old girl is the eldest of Team T-10. May-Trix has hundreds of gadgets and gizmos that she uses to scan her surroundings for exciting data. From analyzing animals' sizes and special abilities, to understanding robotics and space exploration, May-Trix adores it all.

T-10 FILE

There are the *Guardians of the Galaxy*, then there's the Keeper of the Comics... And that's Apollo! This 8-year-old boy is an amazing comic book artist, and knows everything there is to know about superheroes, movies, video games, TV shows and cartoons. He's into sport and outer space, too.

APOLLO

SHAUN VERT

QUANTUM

ZONE 1

All Creatures...

Furry, scaly, feathered, fluffy... We start by looking at ALL creatures great and small!

9

Fish

Did it surprise you to see fish in the top spot? Many people love to look after fish in an aquarium as they are much less costly to keep than a dog or a cat (if you don't buy the very expensive tropical ones). Watching fish can also be very relaxing and good for your mental health.

the lowdown...

MEET MY PET FISH! THIS IS MY CYBORG GOLDFISH CALLED CY-GO.
YOU'LL BE HEARING A LOT MORE FROM US! DID YOU KNOW THE GOLDFISH IS A KIND OF LITTLE CARP? YOU DO NOW!

TOP 10 Most Popular Pets

Are you a cat person or a dog lover? Do your friends prefer aquatic pet-pals? Here's how the stats stack up for the creatures that we most love to have as part of our family.

	PET	POPULARITY*
1	Freshwater Fish	182 MILLION +
2	Cats	96.9 MILLION
3	Dogs	83.1 MILLION
4	Birds	17 MILLION
5	Horses/Ponies	14.1 MILLION
6	Reptiles	13.4 MILLION
7	Saltwater Fish	9.6 MILLION
8	Rabbits	7.1 MILLION
9	Guinea Pigs	2.3 MILLION
10	Hamsters	2.2 MILLION

*UK and US totals combined

CANINE CRAZY!

How many breeds of dog do you think there are? The American Kennel Club recognizes 180 breeds, but with all the cross-breeds in the world, dog fans would say it's more like 400... And growing!

FLUFFY FACT

If you, or someone you know, has a hamster, it's likely it is either a Golden or a Russian Dwarf, as these are the two most popular breeds around the world.

TOP 10 World's Biggest Pets

Prepare to see jumbo sizes that will overload your "What?!"-o-meter!

	PET	NAME	BREED	WEIGHT (KG)	(LB)
1	**Horse**	**Mammoth**	**Shire**	**1,520**	**3,306.9**
2	Pig	Big Bill	Poland China	1,157	2,552
3	Donkey	Romulus	American Mammoth	589.7	1,300
4	Dog	Zorba	Old English Mastiff	155.6	343
5	Snake	Medusa	Reticulated Python	136	300
6	Tortoise	Sammy	African Spurred Tortoise	52.2	115
7	Capybara	Gary	N/A	50.8	112
8	Rabbit	Ralph	Continental Giant	24.9	55
9	Cat	Himmy	Unknown	21.3	46.8
10	Goldfish	Goldie	Goldfish	0.9	2

FLUFFY FACT

Gary the Capybara is the biggest pet rodent in the world! Being semi-aquatic, he enjoys his Texas owners' swimming pool.

ZONE 1: All Creatures...

SIZE 'EM UP

AVERAGE RABBIT
WEIGHT: 2.04 kg (4.5 lb)

WORLD'S BIGGEST RABBIT
WEIGHT: 22.2 kg (49 lb)

the lowdown...

Dog:
English Mastiff

Not quite as big as the heaviest pet pooch, Zorba, THIS English Mastiff called Bentley is still an impressive 102.5 kg (226 lb). Here he is with his proud owner, Dianne Fischer from Newton, Massachusetts.

THE MODERN DOG IS ACTUALLY A DISTANT RELATION OF A KIND OF WOLF THAT EXISTED 30,000 YEARS AGO!

MY FAVORITE DOG? HAS TO BE DOUG FROM THE MOVIE UP.

TOP 10 Longest-Living Pets

We may marvel at our human accomplishments, but never underestimate the natural world. Check out the insanely old ages that these pets can live to!

	PET	NAME	AGE
1	Tortoise	Adwaita	250
2	Koi Carp	Hanako	225
3	Parrot (Macaw)	Charlie	100
4	Horse	Old Billy	62
5	Snake (Ball Python)	Unknown	48
6	Goldfish	Tish	43
7	Cat	Creme Puff	38
8	Dog	Max	26
9	Rabbit	Flopsy	18
10	Chicken	Matilda	15

PARROT

There are more than 370 species of these tropical companions with Cockatoos, Amazons and Macaws living the longest.

Russian Tortoise

These reptiles are very popular pets and a long-term commitment, as you can see by our number one! Russian Tortoises live for at least 50 years, so you're almost guaranteed a four-legged friend who is going to be with you from your schooldays right through to when you're playing bingo with other grandparents!

the lowdown...

TEAM T-10 REPORT

Pet clam, anyone? An Ocean Quohog (a kind of mollusc) that scientists named Ming was an incredible 507 years old when it died in 2006! Not exactly as good at "fetch" as a dog, though. And if you think that age is insane, scientists believe some Sea Glass Sponges may live to be 23,000 years old!

FLUFFY FACT

The word "Koi" is Japanese for "carp." In Japan, what we call Koi Carp are called "Nishikigoi."

the lowdown...

52 MILLION YEARS AGO, EARLY HORSE EOHIPPUS WAS AS SMALL AS A DOG!

Thoroughbred Horse

Fantastically expensive racehorse "The Green Monkey" started his racing career in September 2007 but retired in 2008 at age 4, so he was only actively in competition for 5 months. His unusual name comes from his owners' love of the golf course of the same name in Barbados.

TOP 10 Most Expensive Pets

Now, Team T-10 like pets as much as the next person, but we can't imagine ever saving up the money to splash out on these bank-breaking breeds. Some cost more than several houses!

	ANIMAL	COST ($)
1	Thoroughbred Horse*	15,535,001
2	Racing Pigeons**	5,825,625
3	Tibetan Mastiff	1,844,780
4	Morsan Farm Cow	1,456,405
5	Ram	341,769
6	White Lion Cub	133,988
7	Stag Beetle	86,413
8	Bengal Cat	40,229
9	Lavender Albino Ball Python	38,836
10	Savannah Cat	9,708

Thoroughbred Horse called The Green Monkey
*** Racing Pigeons called Bolt (and Flock)*

MORSAN FARM COW

Ponoka Morsan Farm in Alberta, Canada, trades in the crème de la crème of cows. They are treated in the most organically natural way possible, and one of their most famous sales was "Miss Missy," who went for $1.2 million in 2009!

FLUFFY FACT

White Lion cubs are purchased by super-rich people who want them as exotic pets. BUT these are endangered animals that need our help much more than to be pets: www.whitelionshomeland.org

TOP 10 Richest Pets

Most people leave their money to their kids. But these prosperous pets got rich when their owners died and left them millions!

	NAME	ANIMAL	WORTH ($)
1	**Gunther IV**	**German Shepherd**	**361,188,788**
2	**Toby Rimes**	**Poodle**	**89,326,259**
3	**Kalu**	**Chimpanzee**	**48,219,440**
4	**Luke, Layla, Gracie**	**Dogs**	**29,128,128**
5	**Blackie**	**Cat**	**24,321,766**
6	**Tommaso**	**Cat**	**12,622,188**
7	**Gigoo**	**Hen**	**9,709,376**
=	**Frankie, Ani and Pepe**	**Dog & 2 cats**	**9,709,376**
9	**Pontiac**	**Labrador**	**4,854,688**
10	**Flossie**	**Labrador**	**2,912,812**

TOP DOGS!
Eight dogs feature in the Top 10 Richest Pets... More than any other animal!

TOMMASO USED TO BE A STREET CAT IN ROME BEFORE BECOMING A MULTIMILLIONAIRE!

SIZE 'EM UP

Gunther IV is not doing too badly when you consider that he's as rich as *Transformers*' director Michael Bay and chef Jamie Oliver... And he's a dog!

DOG **GUNTHER IV** *DOG* **TOBY RIMES** *CAT* **BLACKIE** *HEN* **GIGOO**

FLUFFY FACT

Leaving stacks of cash to beloved animals is more common than you think. Queen Elizabeth I left $4.8 million to her cattle and sheep so that they would be properly cared for!

CLUCK CLUCK I'M IN LUCK!

YOU'D THINK TOBY RIMES HAD ROCKSTAR ROOTS, BUT NO... HIS FORTUNE COMES FROM HIS HUMAN FAMILY'S PROPERTY BUSINESS.

the **lowdown**...

Gigoo

Famous publisher Miles Blackwell wasn't sure what to do with his millions after his wife died, so he decided he would pass a large chunk of it to none other than... his pet hen. Talk about the chicken that laid the golden eggs! We figure a fried egg sandwich would cost about $9,708!

TOP 10 Pet-Owning Countries

There are almost 200 countries on Earth, all home to different kinds of animals. But can you guess which 10 are home to the most pets?

WOW... 62 PERCENT OF AMERICAN HOMES INCLUDE A PET!

the lowdown...

	COUNTRY	NUMBER OF PETS (MILLIONS)
1	USA	246.5
2	Brazil	44
3	Russia	42
4	France	32
=	Italy	32
6	China	30
7	Germany	25
8	UK	23
9	Japan	22
10	Philippines	10

USA

Of all those different pets spread across America, 75.8 million of them are dogs. However, in the war of cat and dog fans, the kitties just take the popularity prize – with 76.43 million cats living in American households.

SAMBA PETS!
Sixty percent of Brazilian households have a pet!

France

The 65.8 million people living in France really do love their pets. With 32 million animals having homes, almost half the population owns a pet! It's not surprising that this stat puts France in the top spot for European countries who own the most pets.

DID YOU KNOW THERE ARE 274 SPECIES OF FISH IN GERMANY?

SIZE 'EM UP

Here's how Brazil, France and the UK compare when it comes to how many pets they own...

Each icon represents one million pets

BRAZIL

FRANCE

UK

FLUFFY FACT

Pugs have an incredible history that dates way, way back to China, 700 BC. Great Emperor Ling To (AD 168–190) loved them so much that if you were caught stealing a pug, you would be sentenced to death!

IF I HAD PETS, THEY'D ALL BE CALLED THINGS LIKE GIZMO, GADGET, FLASH AND CHIP!

TEAM T-10 REPORT

The Name Game

Do you have a pet? What about your friends? Why not play a game to see what you would call different animals if you had them as pets, based on some of the more unusual ones you've met so far in this zone. Go!

TOP 10 Most Popular Pet Names

What names have you, or your friends, given your pets? Any really weird ones? See if any of them have made the top 10 most popular ones.

	MALE	FEMALE
1	Dexter	Stella
2	Trapper	Katniss
3	Thor	Bella
4	Bailey	Ellie
5	Winston	Willow
6	Loki	Sophie
7	Hawkeye	Zoey
8	Bentley	Olivia
9	Otto	Lexi
10	Jackson	Sadie

Loki

We can certainly tell that the popularity of the Marvel comic book movies — especially *The Avengers* (2012) — has influenced pets' names! We were hoping for a few Starks though...

the lowdown...

Katniss

The impact of *The Hunger Games* novels and movies on pet-naming is very impressive, considering Katniss (Everdeen) is a very unusual name and specific to that series. Mind you, when you remember the books have sold more than 40 million copies and the movies have made more than $1.5 BILLION, it's not so surprising!

FAME IN A NAME

London has a Walk of Fame dedicated to famous dogs like Lassie and even stop-motion animation legend Gromit, best friend of inventor Wallace. Who are your favorite famous dogs that you'd like to see honored?

MY PETS WOULD DEFINITELY BE CALLED LOKI, THOR AND HAWKEYE, AND I ACTUALLY THINK THAT HULK AND ASGARD ARE AWESOME PET NAMES TOO!

TOP 10 Largest Military Animals

Did you know that animals play a key role in the military services? We think you'll be surprised at some of the types that turn up in this list.

	ANIMAL	ROLE
1	Elephant	Moving heavy equipment
2	Camel	Transporting troops
3	Horse	Has been ridden into battle for 5,000 years
4	Oxen	Carrying heavy supplies over rough terrain
5	Dolphin	Recovering objects in the ocean and mine detection
6	Sea Lion	Recovering objects in the ocean and mine detection
7	Dog	Delivering messages and detection
8	Pig	Used to upset or distract elephants centuries ago
9	Pigeon	Delivering messages
10	Rat	Secret bombs

FLUFFY FACT

Dead rats were filled with explosives and placed in secret places during the Second World War. Yuk!

Pigeons

Pigeons were used by the military to communicate until 1957. They played a very important part due to their speed and incredible navigation skills.

ZONE 1: All Creatures...

SIZE 'EM UP

Here's a handy guide to how these military animals compare...

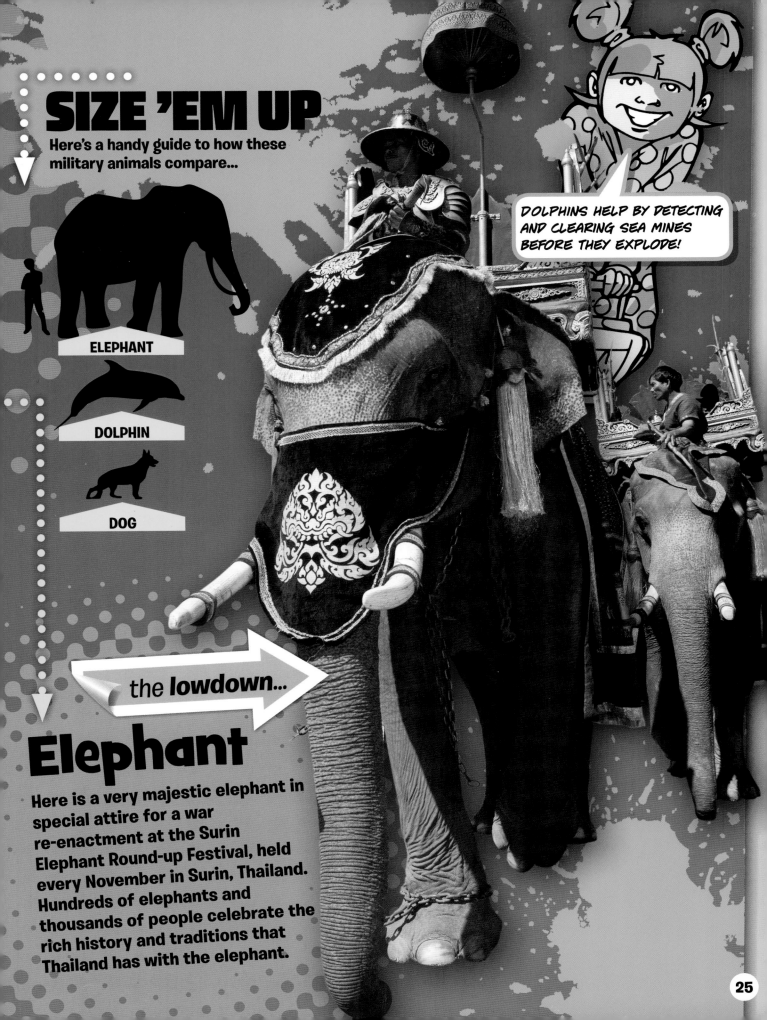

ELEPHANT

DOLPHIN

DOG

DOLPHINS HELP BY DETECTING AND CLEARING SEA MINES BEFORE THEY EXPLODE!

the *lowdown*...

Elephant

Here is a very majestic elephant in special attire for a war re-enactment at the Surin Elephant Round-up Festival, held every November in Surin, Thailand. Hundreds of elephants and thousands of people celebrate the rich history and traditions that Thailand has with the elephant.

ZONE 2

Cats & Dogs

This zone is dedicated to those stick-fetchers and curtain-climbers...

TOP 10 Most Popular Dog Breeds

It's time to settle that argument about which is the most popular kind of dog. These ten are the world's most wanted canines!

BREED

1	Labrador Retriever
2	Yorkshire Terrier
3	German Shepherd
4	Golden Retriever
5	Beagle
6	Boxer
7	Dachshund
8	Cocker Spaniel
9	Poodle
10	Pug

COCKER SPANIEL

These mutts may look super-cute, but behind those adorable eyes lies a much more feisty heritage. The "cocker" in their name comes from the fact that they were originally bred to hunt Woodcocks (a kind of small wading bird).

SIZE 'EM UP

Here's a good visual example of how four of the most popular breeds would look if they were out for a walk together.

GOLDEN RETRIEVER
WEIGHT: 30.8 kg (68 lb)

BOXER
WEIGHT: 30.8 kg (68 lb)

GERMAN SHEPHERD
WEIGHT: 31.8 kg (70 lb)

PUG
WEIGHT: 8.2 kg (18 lb)

THE LABRADOR RETRIEVER IS THE MOST COMMON GUIDE DOG TRAINED TO HELP PARTIALLY SIGHTED AND BLIND PEOPLE.

the **lowdown...**

Labrador Retriever

It's no surprise that these incredible dogs are our overall fave. Labs have amazingly kind personalities and they love to be around people of all ages, from the very young to grandparents. They are also one of the most popular dogs for helping people in therapy and those with sight problems.

FLUFFY **FACT**

The total cost of breeding, training and then supporting a guide dog for its whole working life is around $82,529.

TOP 10 Largest Domestic Cat Breeds

Most kittens tend to be pretty cute little meowing bundles of fluff, but some breeds grow to sizes that put them more in the meow-monster territory.

CAN'T HAVE A CAT BECAUSE THEY MAKE YOU SNEEZE? SOME BREEDERS BELIEVE SIBERIAN CATS ARE HYPOALLERGENIC, WHICH MEANS THEY MIGHT BE SAFE PETS FOR ALLERGY SUFFERERS.

	BREED	AVERAGE WEIGHT (KG)	(LB)
1	Savannah	11.3	25
2	Maine Coon	7.7	17
3	British Shorthair	7.5	16.5
4	Ragdoll	7.3	16
5	Ragamuffin	7	15.5
6	Norwegian Forest	6.4	14
7	Siberian	6.1	13.5
8	Chausie	5.4	12
=	American Shorthair	5.4	12
10	American Bobtail	5	11

the lowdown...

Savannah Cat

These domestic cat-wildcat cross-breeds are very energetic, and can leap as high as 2.4 m (8 ft) from a standing still position! Savannah owners often talk about how their cats behave more like dogs, and Savannahs can be trained to walk on a lead and play games. Unlike most domestic cats, they enjoy being in water.

TALK ABOUT AWESOME HYBRIDS. THE SAVANNAH IS PART DOMESTIC CAT, PART AFRICAN WILDCAT!

Ragdoll

These are lovable and dopey but very strong cats. They got given their name because when you pick them up, they become very relaxed and floppy.

FLUFFY FACT

Back in Ancient Egyptian times, cats were considered very sacred animals. Some even got mummified after they died!

TOP 10 Smallest Dog Breeds

How much is that doggie in the window? You know, that one there... No THERE... The one so small it could be mistaken for a hamster!

	BREED	WEIGHT (KG)	(LB)
1	Pomeranian	2.3	5
2	Yorkshire Terrier	2.5	5.5
3	Chihuahua	3.2	6
4	Toy Poodle	3.4	7.5
5	Papillon	3.9	8.5
6	Shih Tzu	5.9	13
7	Bichon Frisé	6.8	15
8	Pug	8.2	18
=	Boston Terrier	8.2	18
10	French Bulldog	10.7	23.5

MINIATURE MUTTS!
There are lots of reasons that small dog breeds are so popular. Apart from the fact that they cost less to feed and look after, they also need less exercise and are accepted into hotels more often. Something that might surprise you is that small dogs generally live longer than larger breeds, with some exceeding 15 years of age.

SIZE 'EM UP
Here's how some of the top 10 smallest dogs compare. Don't be deceived by the bulky coat of the Pomeranian. Underneath all that it's tiny!

POMERANIAN
WEIGHT: 2.3 kg (5 lb)

CHIHUAHUA
WEIGHT: 3.2 kg (6 lb)

TOY POODLE
WEIGHT: 3.4 kg (7.5 lb)

PUG
WEIGHT: 8.2 kg (18 lb)

FLUFFY **FACT**

Chihuahua cross-breeds aside, the official kennel clubs of the world only recognize two kinds – the Long-haired and Short-haired. Both can live as long as 20 years!

THE SMALLEST DOG IN THE WORLD IS A CHIHUAHUA NAMED MILLY. SHE IS 9.65 CM (3.8 IN) TALL AND WEIGHS 0.45 KG (1 LB).

the **lowdown**...

Chihuahua

These little dogs have a very intriguing past. Scientists know the breed began in Mexico (they're named after the state of Chihuahua), and believe they're related to ancient companion dogs called the Techichi, which were first recorded in the 9th century.

IF YOU'RE LOOKING FOR A TINY PET WITH ROYAL APPROVAL, TRY A POMERANIAN. BRITISH MONARCH QUEEN VICTORIA HAD A POMERANIAN AND MADE THEM A POPULAR CHOICE DURING HER REIGN.

TOP 10 Smallest Domestic Cat Breeds

A kitten can melt your heart with its big eyes and clumsy ways, but imagine if your adult cat was still pretty much the same sit-in-your-palm size as when it was a baby!

FLUFFY FACT

Singapura cats love to sit up very high, so they can survey their surroundings. They're famous for their blunt-ended tails.

Singapura INFO

ACTIVITY LEVEL	3
INTELLIGENCE	4
CURIOSITY	4
FRIENDLINESS	3
VOLUME LEVEL	2

BREED	WEIGHT (KG)	(LB)
1 Dwelf	1.8	4
2 Minskin	2.3	5
= Kinkalow	2.3	5
= Skookum	2.3	5
5 Singapura	2.7	6
6 Lambkin	2.9	6.5
7 Bambino	3.2	7
= Napoleon	3.2	7
9 Munchkin	3.4	7.5
= Cornish Rex	3.4	7.5

TEAM **T-10** REPORT

Missed by a whisker

There are other tiny kitties that just missed out on a place in this top 10: LaPerm, Peterbald, Tonkinese, Devon Rex, Abyssinian, American Curl, Bombay and Burmese, with average weights ranging from 3.6–5.2 kg (8–11.5 lb).

PURRFECT PET

Did you know that stroking and cuddling fluffy pets like cats is good for your health? It reduces stress and tension and can lower blood pressure too!

the lowdown...

CATFIGHT!
Cats in the USA kill nearly 4 billion birds every year!

Singapura

Their unusual name comes from the Malay word for Singapore, which is where this breed originated from. It was only in 1981 that they were legally and officially accepted into the USA for breeding and ownership. They may be small, but they have a tough and stocky build.

SINGAPURA
WEIGHT: 2.7 kg (6 lb)

AVERAGE CAT
WEIGHT: 3.9 kg (8.6 lb)

TOP 10 Biggest Dog Breeds

Is it a dog, or a HORSE?! These relatives of the wolf would actually make a wild canine quiver. Surely some of these breeds could be used as transport instead of cycling to school?

	BREED	HEIGHT (CM)	(IN)
1	Irish Wolfhound	86.4	34
2	Pyrenean Mountain Dog	81.3	32
3	Leonberger	80	31.5
4	Neapolitan Mastiff	78.7	31
5	Great Dane	76.2	30
6	Newfoundland	71.1	28
7	Saint Bernard	69.9	27.5
=	Bernese Mountain Dog	69.9	27.5
9	Bull Mastiff	68.6	27
=	Dogue de Bordeaux	68.6	27

THE HOWLING
The number one's name comes from the fact that it used to hunt wolves!

Bull Mastiff
Back in the 19th century these dogs were used as guards to protect the estates of the wealthy. Don't be fooled by their tough appearance, though, as they don't often bark and are very sensitive.

SIZE 'EM UP
These two breeds are pretty close in terms of height! Here's how their profiles compare...

IRISH WOLFHOUND
HEIGHT: 86.4 cm (34 in)

BULL MASTIFF
HEIGHT: 68.6 cm (27 in)

THIS DOG-ZILLA CAN WEIGH UP TO A WHOPPING 77.1 KG (170 LB)!

the **lowdown**...

Leonberger

Despite their huge size and presence, these mountain dogs have a very gentle, caring nature. With their thick and waterproof coats, you can see why they're used as rescue dogs. They can also pull carts!

TOP 10 Most Expensive Cat Breeds

Let's say that you love cats. Let's say you REALLY love cats. Could you ever see yourself splashing out the cash for any of these breeds?

	BREED	HIGHEST COST ($)
1	Ashera	96,973
2	Savannah	48,525
3	Bengal	24,262
4	Allerca	5,822
5	Persian	5,337
6	Peterbald	4,851
7	Russian Blue	2,911
=	Sphynx	2,911
=	Scottish Fold	2,911
10	British Shorthair	1,455

PETERBALD

This Russian breed has a very unusual genetic detail. It loses its hair. If a Peterbald (the clue's in the name) is born with some hair, due to its genetic make-up its hair will eventually drop out.

THE RUSSIAN BLUE IS KNOWN FOR ITS SILVER-BLUE COAT, BRIGHT GREEN EYES AND FRIENDLY NATURE.

ME AND CY-GO TIME-TRAVELED TO LONDON, UK, IN 1871 TO SEE THE FIRST PERSIAN CAT COMPETE IN A CAT SHOW!

DID YOU KNOW THAT ASHERA CATS HAVE BEEN SPECIALLY BRED TO LOOK LIKE MINI LEOPARDS?

the lowdown...

Persian Cat

This ridiculously cute furball is the most popular cat of all breeds in the USA. The quiet and gentle feline's super-fluffy fur needs to be bathed and groomed often to keep it clean... Unfortunately, this is not something most cats enjoy!

FLUFFY FACT

A popular trend among Persian owners is to shave their cat's fur (except on their heads) to keep them cool, or simply to be fashionable. Perfect for copycats who want to look like their human owners!

TOP 10 Most Popular Cat Names

Do you or one of your friends have a cat? Maybe its name is featured on this list of the names cat owners most love to call their kitties.

	MALE	FEMALE
1	Sam	Bella
2	Max	Misty
3	Tigger	Kitty
4	Charlie	Princess
5	Sooty	Chloe
6	Smokey	Lily
7	Lucky	Puss
8	Leo	Fluffy
9	Simba	Molly
10	Smudge	Daisy

the lowdown...

Bella

The *Twilight* series of books and movies, created by author Stephenie Meyer, have had a huge impact on popular culture and pet names. The name of the main female character in the *Twilight* tales is Bella Swan.

POP STAR KATY PERRY OWNS A MAINE COON CAT CALLED KITTY PURRY!

Copycats

Based on our calculations of the recorded cat population in some countries, we estimate that across the whole planet there are over 500 million pet cats in human homes!

FLUFFY FACT

One of the most timeless names for a pet cat is Kitty; however, it is very rare for a pet dog to be named Puppy/Doggie.

Wacky Names

Believe it or not these are real names that owners have given to their cats.

SASSY PANTS HUSKA
KITTY GAGA
MISTER BIGGLESWORTH
MAGNIFICAT
MR CHUBSY BUTTONS
TIGER BLOOD
ALBUS DUMBLEDORE

BLACK SABBATH
CUDDLES MCCRACKEN
KITTY BOWERSOCKS
KAHLUA FUDGE
SCHNICKELFRITZ
BEANBAG
DUMPSTER KITTY

TOP 10

Most Expensive Dog Breeds

Dogs are awesome, but if you have your heart set on having a certain breed as part of your family, sadly it might require a LOT of saving up first...

	BREED	HIGHEST COST ($)
1	Samoyed	10,674
2	English Bulldog	8,732
3	Chow Chow	8,248
4	Lowchen	7,761
=	Rottweiler	7,761
6	Tibetan Mastiff	6,792
7	Pharaoh Hound	6,306
8	Akita	4,366
9	Bearded Collie	4,850
10	Saluki	2,424

SIZE 'EM UP

SAMOYED — PHARAOH HOUND

TIBETAN MASTIFF

Although this breed makes an excellent pet, they were originally bred to protect livestock and are stil used in this way in some countries. They are so powerful that they will even ward off wolves!

DON'T WORRY THOUGH, NOT ALL DOGS COST THOUSANDS. FOR EXAMPLE, AN ENGLISH FOXHOUND PUP CAN BE BOUGHT FOR AS LITTLE AS $50.

THEY MAY OFTEN LOOK LIKE TOUGH CUSTOMERS, BUT ENGLISH BULLDOGS ARE ACTUALLY VERY GENTLE.

the lowdown...

English Bulldog

This iconic dog breed has been adopted as a mascot by many organizations over the past several decades. From the military to universities, and even through to professional sports teams like the Boston Bulldogs, this loveable and bold-faced canine remains as popular as ever.

FLUFFY FACT

English Bulldogs make great pets if you live in an apartment without a backyard because they love to laze around. But it's still important, as with all dogs, to give them daily walks.

Pharaoh Hound

Although this Maltese hound looks like its roots lie in Ancient Egypt, it actually has no genetic connection to that era or location. Its official name, "Kalb tal-Fenek," describes its appearance: "rabbit dog."

MY FAVE DOG NAMES ARE ALL ABOUT SPEED: ROCKET, WHIZZER, SCOOTER AND JET ARE DEFINITELY EXAMPLES OF WHAT I'D NAME MY PUP!

FLUFFY FACT

If you're not sure what name to give your pup, there are lots of useful pet websites that can suggest names based on your dog's personality.

TOP 10 Most Popular Dog Names

When you're out in the park, you'll hear dog owners calling out for their canine chums. How many of these names do you regularly come across?

TEAM T-10 REPORT

Name that hound

People choose names for their pets based on many different factors. Usually it's a combination of the animal's personality and appearance, and also a reference to something the owner loves, like a movie or TV character.

the lowdown...

	MALE	FEMALE
1	Max	Bella
2	Bailey	Lucy
3	Charlie	Daisy
4	Jack	Molly
5	Cooper	Ruby
6	Buddy	Maggie
7	Toby	Sadie
8	Bear	Chloe
9	Jake	Lola
10	Buster	Bailey

Bailey

Well, look at that – Bailey has a spot on both the male and female lists. The name is actually unisex, meaning it can be used for both boys and girls.

Wacky Names

Believe it or not, these are real names that owners have given to their dogs...

CHEW BARKA
CAPTAIN AWESOME
NACHO CHEESE
MONSTER TRUCK MICKEY
MR CASHEW MAGHOO
SANTA PAWS
ZOOLANDER

DIXON BAINBRIDGE
BOOGIE WOOGIE
OREO-DUNKIN
SNAZZEL
FUDGE MCDREAMY
SPARK PUG
AGENT 99

TOP 10 Unusual Dog Breeds

Here we've tracked down 10 of the most extraordinary-looking breeds on the planet. Some look like they should be cartoon characters!

BREED

1	**Chinese Crested**
2	Xoloitzcuintli
3	Peruvian Inca Orchid
4	Puli
5	Bedlington Terrier
6	Shar Pei
7	Brussels Griffon
8	Neapolitan Mastiff
9	Bergamasco Shepherd
10	English Bull Terrier

ARCHAEOLOGICAL DISCOVERIES SUGGEST THAT THE SHAR PEI BREED MAY BE 2,500 YEARS OLD!

Shar Pei

These rare dogs have loads of chunky wrinkles, which give them a striking look but can cause ear problems. Their tongues are an unusual blue-black color, too.

SIZE 'EM UP

Standing at similar heights, the English Bull Terrier is around 31.8 kg (70 lb), with the Shar Pei at 24 kg (53 lb).

ENGLISH BULL TERRIER   **SHAR PEI**

THE PULI BREED HAS AN AMAZING LONG CORDED COAT THAT LOOKS SIMILAR TO DREADLOCKS.

FLUFFY FACT

The Xoloitzcuintli is also known as the Mexican Hairless dog. The breed's shortened name is Xolo, and owners often describe their behavior as very playful. They're also great climbers.

the lowdown...

Chinese Crested

Although they're branded one of the "hairless" dog breeds, as you can see, they do have hair. But it's only in certain places, which gives them their funny style! The Powderpuff type actually has a full body of hair.

WHIPPET

This breed looks very similar to the Greyhound because they are related – Whippets are a decendant breed. Smaller at 11.3 kg (25 lb), they are not as fast, but they hold the title for the quickest acceleration.

KRYPTO WAS A VERY SUPER DOG... HE WAS SUPERMAN'S PET! HE FIRST APPEARED IN A 1955 DC COMICS BOOK.

TOP 10 Fastest Dog Breeds

Our four-legged friends can certainly whip along at terrific speeds when they want to. Out of all the breeds, these 10 race along the fastest. Some get near a cheetah's speed!

	BREED	TOP SPEED (KM/H)	(MPH)
1	Greyhound	69.2	43
2	Saluki	64.3	40
=	Vizsla	64.3	40
4	Dalmatian	60	37
5	Borzoi	57.9	36
6	Weimaraner	56.3	35
=	Whippet	56.3	35
8	Doberman Pinscher	48.3	30
=	Border Collie	48.3	30
10	Russell Terrier	40.2	25

AVERAGING AROUND 30.8 KG (68 LB), A GREYHOUND IS PURE MUSCLE WITH A HUGE, POWERFUL HEART.

the lowdown...

Greyhound

These dogs are built for speed, so it comes as no surprise that Greyhound racing has been a very popular sport (for either gambling events, or just for fun) in several countries for over 100 years.

Saluki

Also known as the Persian Greyhound. the Saluki is thought by many experts to be an ancient breed of dog. Artwork on rocks that are 10.000 years old shows dogs that look very Saluki-esque.

TOP 10 Smartest Dog Breeds

People who love and know dogs will often talk about how smart they are. Here are 10 breeds that are known for being super-intelligent.

	BREED	QUALITIES
1	Border Collie	Sheep herders with amazing instinct
2	Labrador Retriever	Kind, caring dogs who are easy to train
3	Bloodhound	Experts at following a scent in detection work
4	German Shepherd	Intelligent dogs used by the police and military
5	Doberman Pinscher	Clever breed who quickly learn obedience commands
6	Belgian Malinois	Military dogs who are easily trained
7	Australian Shepherd	Herding dogs who love to learn new skills
8	Siberian Husky	Sled-pullers with great endurance and strength
9	Beagle	Use their strong sense of smell to detect bedbugs
10	Poodle	Hardworking and have a high level of obedience

the **lowdown...**

▶ Poodle

Each of the three poodle types – Standard, Miniature, and Toy – are known for their intelligence as much as their super-fluffy, sheep-like coats. Being so smart, they get bored very easily, so it's important that owners spend a lot of time playing with them.

ONE OF THE WORLD'S MOST FAMOUS BEAGLES IS SNOOPY OF THE COMIC STRIP "PEANUTS."

FLUFFY FACT

Two Border Collie dog actors starred as sheepdogs Fly and Rex in the two *Babe* movies from 1995 and 1998.

Border Collie
INFO

ADAPTABILITY					3
TRAINABILITY					5
HEALTH & GROOMING					3
FRIENDLINESS					4
EXERCISE NEEDS					5

Doberman Pinscher

These dogs have a very striking look and their history dates back to the end of the 19th century. when they were guard dogs to protect tax collectors. They have also been cast in many scary movies. although they actually have a very obedient and loyal temperament.

BLOODHOUNDS HAVE AN INCREDIBLE SENSE OF SMELL AND CAN STILL PICK OUT HUMAN ODORS LEFT BEHIND DAYS AGO. THEY CAN EVEN TRACK A SCENT OVER WATER.

ZONE 3

Cute & Fluffy

If it's adorable to look at, it'll be in this zone...

TOP 10 Cutest Pets

There are countless animals that are beyond super-cute, so Team T-10 found it a tricky challenge to select the 10 cutest for you. But we're very happy with this list!

	NAME	TYPE
1	**Fennec Fox**	North African Fox
2	**Boston Terrier**	Dog
3	**Netherland Dwarf**	Rabbit
4	**Chinchilla**	Rodent
5	**British Shorthair**	Cat
6	**Box Turtle**	Turtle
7	**Ferret**	Weasel
8	**American Crested**	Guinea Pig
9	**Miniature Pig**	Pig
10	**Gecko**	Lizard

British Shorthair

Not only is this breed of cat really chilled out and sociable, but it's also a clever kitty that can learn small tricks. You might see British Shorthairs acting in movies and TV ads.

SIZE 'EM UP

To give you more of an idea of how these pets' sizes compare to one another, here's an at-a-glance view of how they would look if they were standing in the same yard.

CHINCHILLA
WEIGHT: 0.6 kg (1.35 lb)

NETHERLAND DWARF
WEIGHT: 0.9 kg (2 lb)

BOSTON TERRIER
WEIGHT: 8.2 kg (18 lb)

FLUFFY FACT

Although having a Miniature Pig as a pet has become really popular, be careful, as there is no way to be 100 percent sure the pig you've bought will stay tiny.

MINIATURE PIGS ARE SMART SO CAN BE HOUSE-TRAINED LIKE CATS AND DOGS.

THE FENNEC FOX LIVES IN THE SAHARA DESERT, SO THE SOLES OF ITS FEET ARE PROTECTED FROM THE HOT DESERT SAND BY A THICK LAYER OF FUR.

the lowdown...

Fennec Fox

These insanely cute furballs make great pet companions, but remember that because they're wild animals (and not domesticated like cats and dogs), they need a LOT more attention. They make a variety of sounds including barking like a dog and purring like a cat!

TOP 10 Funniest Long-Haired Pets

If you or one of your friends has a pet, how crazy is its hairdo? We bet it doesn't come anywhere near the level of bonkers reached by these animals' styles.

	NAME	TYPE
1	Bergamasco	Dog
2	Pygmy Goat	Goat
3	Long-Haired Syrian	Hamster
4	Persian	Cat
5	Lionhead	Rabbit
6	Silkie	Guinea Pig
7	Longhair Astrex	Mouse
=	Lhasa Apso	Dog
9	Llama	Camelid
10	Himalayan	Cat

Bergamasco

You'd be forgiven for thinking that this breed was a bit scruffy, but the Bergamasco's striking coat is completely normal. It's made up of three types of hair: a fine, oily undercoat, a woolly topcoat and longer, coarse hairs. This third type weaves together as the dog gets older to form flat mats or flocks.

PYGMY ANIMALS ARE TINY VERSIONS OF BIGGER BREEDS. PYGMY GOATS ARE NOT MUCH LARGER THAN CATS!

Lionhead

If you want to own the absolute fluffiest version possible of a Lionhead, then you'll want to go for the "double mane" breed. These have extra-crazy fluffy tufts around their neck and body.

the lowdown...

FLUFFY FACT

Would a Pygmy Goat be your dream pet? If so, they come in several different colors including a range of caramel tones, and also the classic silvery-grey goat color.

SHED LLAMA HAIR IS USED TO MAKE ROPE, RUGS AND EVEN CLOTHING!

TOP 10

Smallest Rabbit Breeds

Bunnies! Really, REALLY tiny bunnies! Team T-10 loves rabbits, and so investigating which kinds are the tiniest was a a fun and fluffy job.

	BREED	AVERAGE (KG)	(LB)
1	Netherland Dwarf	0.9	2
2	Britannia Petite	1	2.25
3	Dwarf Hotot	1.3	2.5
=	Polish	1.3	2.5
5	Jersey Woolly	1.6	3.5
=	Mini Plush Lop	1.6	3.5
=	American Fuzzy Lop	1.6	3.5
8	Lionhead	1.7	3.75
9	Holland Lop	1.8	4
=	Himalayan	1.8	4

FLUFFY FACT

How many different breeds of rabbit do you think there are? Would you have guessed anywhere near as many as 48?! If you did, then you definitely know your bunnies.

SIZE 'EM UP

Here's a guide to how three of the smallest bunnies measure up against each other...

NETHERLAND DWARF
WEIGHT: 0.9 kg (2 lb)

MINI PLUSH LOP
WEIGHT: 1.6 kg (3.5 lb)

HIMALAYAN
WEIGHT: 1.8 kg (4 lb)

NURALAGUS REX LIVED MILLIONS OF YEARS AGO. IT WAS A MONSTROUS 11.8 KG (26 LB) RELATIVE OF MODERN BUNNIES.

ZONE 3: Cute & Fluffy

58

Netherland Dwarfs are super-smart and can be house-trained like dogs and cats.

Britannia Petite

Owners of Britannia Petites often say that they love to show off, so they make fantastically playful pet buddies. The breed comes in lots of different kinds, including our fave, the Black Otter Britannia Petite. This bunny has a black body and white belly, very similar to the markings of a River Otter, so they ROCK!

the lowdown...

Netherland Dwarf

Unlike the famous image of Bugs Bunny munching on a carrot, Netherland Dwarfs have very sensitive tummies and should not be fed fresh vegetables. Instead, they need to eat special dry pellets and lots of hay.

BUGS BUNNY STARRED IN HIS FIRST ANIMATED TALE, "A WILD HARE," WAY, WAY BACK IN 1940! IT EVEN GOT NOMINATED FOR AN ACADEMY AWARD.

TIME TO SNOOZE
Chipmunks sleep for an average of 15 hours a day!

CHIPMUNKS ARE VERY FAST FOR THEIR SIZE - THEY CAN RUN AT UP TO 33 KM/H (20.5 MPH)!

the lowdown...

Chipmunk

Chipmunks call North America home, with the exception of the Siberian Chipmunk, which lives in parts of Asia. In the wild they can build their burrows by tunnelling more than 3.5 m (11.4 ft). That's why they need lots of tubes and pipes when kept as pets.

TOP 10 Smallest Rodent Pets

Are you a mouse fan? A hamster lover? Then you'll be pleased that those little creatures are high up on this chart of tiny four-legged pals that we love to look after

	ANIMAL	AVERAGE WEIGHT (G)	(OZ)
1	Mouse	17	0.6
2	Chipmunk	85	3
3	Gerbil	100	3.5
4	Hamster	113.4	4
5	Sugar Glider	120	4.2
6	Degus	235	8.3
7	Rat	450	15.9
8	Chinchilla	600	21.2
9	Guinea Pig	900	31.7
10	Agouti	3,991.6	140.8

Degus

Deguses are very affectionate pets and will often groom their owners to bond with them! Like dogs and cats, they recognize who they know and will get very excited when they approach them.
Too cute!

ALTHOUGH GENETICALLY UNRELATED, THE CHINCHILLA RABBIT WAS BRED SPECIALLY TO LOOK LIKE... A CHINCHILLA!

G-FORCE!

CGI (computer-generated imagery) Guinea Pigs became the stars of the 2009 spy comedy, *G-Force*. The gadget-toting FBI pet agents took a massive $293 million at the box office!

TOP 10 Cutest Baby Animals

Team T-10 is about to present to you a list of newborns that we think beat pretty much all other baby creatures on the cuteness front. If you don't recognize some of them, seek them out!

DON'T WORRY, CY-GO, MOST OWLS PREFER TO HUNT FOR SMALL MAMMALS AND INSECTS, RATHER THAN FISH!

THE SEAL POINT SIAMESE IS A BREED OF CAT AS WELL AS BREED OF MOUSE – WE HOPE THEY NEVER MEET!

	ANIMAL	TYPE
1	African Pygmy Hedgehog	Hedgehog
2	Bichon Frisé	Dog
3	Northern Saw-Whet	Owl
4	Cayuga Duck	Duck
5	American Shorthair	Cat
6	Seal Point Siamese	Mouse
7	Miniature Arabian Horse	Horse
8	Potbellied Pig	Pig
9	Campbell's Dwarf	Hamster
10	Terrapin	Turtle

Happy hoglets

There can be as many as six baby hoglets in an adult hedgehog's litter. Although they're small mammals, hedgehogs can live for more than 7 years. Their ability to roll into a spiky ball is a great defence against predators.

Northern Saw-Whet

In North America it's likely you'll hear this bird at night as it's one of this region's most common owls. If you've read the novel *Guardians of Ga'Hoole* by Kathryn Lasky, you'll know it features a Northern Saw-Whet called Martin.

FLUFFY FACT

This kind of duck gets its fancy name from the Cayuga Lake (in New York) where it was originally bred.

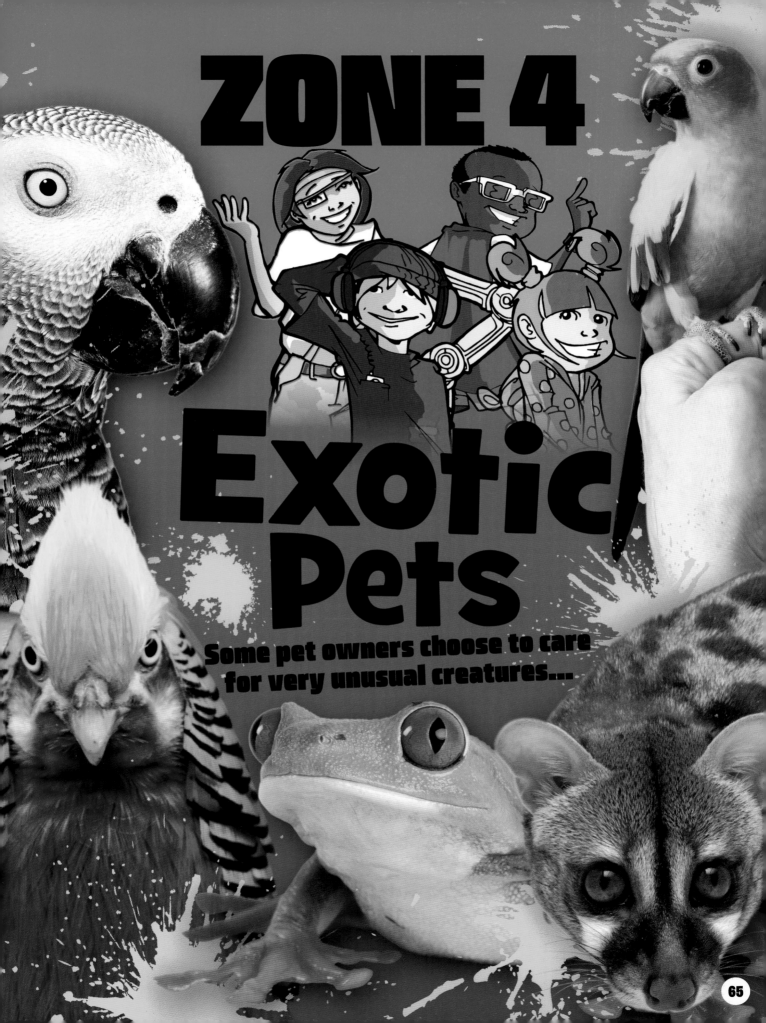

ZONE 4

Exotic Pets

Some pet owners choose to care for very unusual creatures...

TOP 10 Weirdest Exotic Pets

For those pet lovers out there who aren't content to look after a cat or a dog, there are lots of unusual creatures that have become unexpected pets.

Giant African Land Snail

They aren't the cuddliest of the exotic pets in this list, but some people find these molluscs fascinating. Their shells can grow to a massive 30 cm (11.8 in).

ANIMAL

1	**Tamandua**
2	**Boa Constrictor**
3	**Spotted Genet**
4	**Stick Insect**
5	**Axolotl**
6	**Potbellied Pig**
7	**Madagascar Hissing Cockroach**
8	**Kinkajou**
9	**Bearded Dragon**
10	**Giant African Land Snail**

SIZE 'EM UP

Here are three very different exotic pets to show how their sizes compare...

TAMANDUA
LENGTH: 60 cm (23 in)

AXOLOTL
LENGTH: 24 cm (9.5 in)

KINKAJOU
LENGTH: 49.5 cm (19.5 in)

the lowdown...

Spotted Genet

These very striking-looking mammals are popular exotic pets. Owners say they are curious and playful and love to climb. They are also very loyal to their adopted human family and form a strong bond with them.

TEAM T-10 REPORT

The snake man!

Florida resident Albert Killian REALLY loves snakes. He shares his apartment with no less than 60 of them! Albert sensibly has notes next to each of the venomous snakes' cases with their anti-venom info.

TOP 10 Smallest Popular Pet Primates

Be prepared for plenty of monkeying around if you like the idea of tiny primates as pets. They may be small but they are VERY demanding...

CHECK OUT THE HANDLEBAR MOUSTACHE ON THE EMPEROR TAMARIN! THESE MONKEYS WERE ROCKING THIS LOOK WAY BEFORE THE 18TH-CENTURY WILD WEST ERA OF THE USA.

	TYPE	HEAD-BODY LENGTH		TOTAL LENGTH (INC. TAIL)	
		(CM)	(IN)	(CM)	(IN)
1	Pygmy Marmoset	11.7	4.6	28.4	11.2
2	Common Marmoset	17.8	7	35.6	14
3	Black Tamarin	20.3	8	45.7	18
4	Emperor Tamarin	19.8	7.8	46.5	18.3
5	Rhesus Macaque	38.1	15	55.9	22
6	White-Faced Capuchin	30.5	12	61	24
7	Common Squirrel	30.5	12	71.1	28
8	Grivet	45.7	18	95.3	37.5
9	Brown-Faced Spider	30.5	12	99	39
10	Vervet	45.7	18	104	41

GRIVET

The Grivet is very active in the morning and early evening. It loves to play, so daring exotic pet owners have to be prepared to have a LOT of space for it to monkey around in.

FLUFFY FACT
The Pygmy Marmoset eats bark gum from the trees in its Amazon home.

A RHESUS MONKEY CALLED ABLE WAS ONE OF THE FIRST ANIMALS TO BE SENT INTO SPACE!

the lowdown...

Pygmy Marmoset

As small as this mini-monkey may be, it has some amazing leaping skills. It can easily jump 5 m (16 ft) between branches! It is also famous for the range of chirps and bleats it uses to communicate.

TOP 10 Most Fabulous Birds

With countless birds sporting feathers that rival a rainbow, this list was tricky to do, but these 10 are definitely some of the most bright and beautiful.

TYPE

1	**Golden Pheasant**
2	**Mandarin Duck**
3	**Apricot-Headed Caique**
4	**Turaco**
5	**Sun Conure**
6	**Gold & Blue Macaw**
7	**Rainbow Lorikeet**
8	**Rose-Breasted Cockatoo**
9	**Peacock**
10	**Toucan**

Sun Conure

These gorgeous birds live for up to 30 years. They are very easy to train if you give them plenty of love and attention, and they like to have lots of space to fly and explore. They get their name from the way a flock was once described as a sunset moving across the sky.

150 MILLION YEARS AGO, THE SKIES WERE HOME TO ARCHAEOPTERYX. IT BRIDGED THE EVOLUTIONARY GAP BETWEEN REPTILES AND BIRDS.

Golden Pheasant

Does this fancy-pants bird look like a Disney Pixar character or what?! The Golden Pheasant originally hails from the mountains of China, but populations have been introduced into the UK, and elsewhere too. It can take off and fly a little, but this bird is happier on the ground.

the lowdown...

SOME BIRDS' STRIKING APPEARANCE HELPS ATTRACT A MATE, AND ALSO PUTS PREDATORS OFF ATTACKING THEM.

FLUFFY FACT

Fans of exotic birds have to be careful which species they buy, as they might get a BIG shock at the cost. For example, a Hyacinth Macaw will break the bank with a $11,592 price tag!

DID YOU KNOW?
Some species of Toucan have a beak that's longer than half their body length!

TOP 10 Cleverest Pet Birds

The word "birdbrain" refers to someone who is not being very clever. The reality is that birds are WAY more intelligent than that suggests, and these popular pet birds are super-smart.

	TYPE	EVIDENCE
1	African Grey Parrot	Intelligence can rival a 5-year-old child
2	Macaw	Has the emotional maturity of a 2-year-old child
3	Cockatoo	Can pick locks and solve difficult puzzles
4	Crow	Can communicate and work together
5	Magpie	Mourns for members of the flock that die
6	Budgerigar	Requires smart toys and games for stimulation
7	Green Amazon	Reputation for having complex personalities
8	Parakeet	Has the intelligence of a 3-year-old child
9	Quaker Parrot	Learns and uses human language correctly
10	Canary	Incredible "singers" and learners

SIZE 'EM UP

These two birds are very popular pets, so let's see how their sizes compare.

COCKATOO
LENGTH: 30–60 cm (12–24 in)

CANARY
LENGTH: 10–20 cm (4–8 in)

FLUFFY FACT

Crows are incredibly smart. They can remember faces, and be trained to solve complex puzzles. They also use tools to get what they want, using sticks to reach for food. They work regularly on movie sets, and TV shows and commercials as well.

THESE PARROTS ARE VERY SENSITIVE SOULS, AND ARE FAMOUS FOR COPYING THINGS THEIR OWNERS SAY.

BRAINS

Do not underestimate the braininess of a bird. Compared to the mass of its body, a bird has a BIG brain – not that different in ratio terms to big primates.

African Grey Parrot

the lowdown...

This 400 g (0.9 lb) bird will eat insects, but its fave foods are nuts, fruits and leaves. It will also nibble on flowers and tree bark when it can. The African Grey is so smart it is often called the Einstein of the bird world (after renowned physicist Albert Einstein).

TEAM T-10 REPORT

Professor Parrot

There is an amazing documentary called *Life With Alex* (the name of an African Grey Parrot), looking at how he interacted with Dr. Irene Pepperberg and her colleague Arlene Levin-Rowe: www.lifewithalexmovie.com

TOP 10 Most Popular Nocturnal Pets

When choosing a pet, it's important to know which ones are more active at night – otherwise they might keep you awake if they're staying in your bedroom!

PUTTING A SPECIAL BAT BOX ON YOUR OUTSIDE WALL HELPS BATS NEST! DON'T TOUCH THEM, BUT THEY'RE GREAT TO WATCH.

THE WORD "NOCTURNAL" DESCRIBES AN ANIMAL THAT IS MORE ACTIVE DURING OUR BEDTIME THAN IN THE DAY.

FLUFFY FACT

Just like a Kangaroo, the Sugar Glider is a marsupial that begins its life inside its mother's tummy pouch. Despite humans being giants to them, they are very affectionate to their owners.

ANIMAL	
1	**Hamster**
2	Mouse
3	Rat
4	Gerbil
5	Chinchilla
6	Leopard Gecko
7	Sugar Glider
8	Red-Eyed Tree Frog
9	Ball Python
10	African Pygmy Hedgehog

SIZE 'EM UP

Here's a handy visual guide that shows the size comparisons between some of the most popular nocturnal pets...

SIZE OF A TENNIS BALL

HAMSTER

CHINCHILLA

LEOPARD GECKO

GERBIL

RAT

Rat idol!

Rats are worshipped in the Karni Mata Temple in Rajasthan, India! Thousands of the rodents dwell inside and are given a LOT of love, care and food, because many residents believe they are the descendants of an incarnation of the goddess Durga.

the lowdown...

Red-Eyed Tree Frog

These Central American amphibians are very popular with fans of exotic pets. They love company, and are much happier in pairs or groups. Their Latin name, *Agalychnis callidryas*, means "beautiful tree nymph."

DID YOU KNOW?
Chinchillas need a LOT of exercise, so make sure you can provide that before getting one.

TOP 10 Most Beautiful Tropical Fish

This was a hard list to complete, simply because there are so many stunning tropical fish. Go to your local aquarium, and you'll see! These are 10 that we feel deserve a special mention.

TYPE

1	Emperor Angelfish
2	Bumblebee Goby
3	Clownfish
4	Neon Tetra Jumbo
5	Figure Eight Puffer
6	Mono Sebae
7	Blue Diamond Discus
8	Marble Veil Angelfish
9	Crown Tail Betta
10	Clown Loach

Emperor Angelfish

This magnificent fish needs a lot of room inside a tank: at least 833 liters (220 gallons) of water. It also needs a lot of caves and rocks because, just like in the wild, it likes to hide – that makes it feel safe.

the lowdown...

A YOUNG EMPEROR ANGELFISH ACTUALLY STARTS OUT BLACK WITH WHITE AND BLUE STRIPES, AND CHANGES COLOR AS IT BECOMES AN ADULT.

THAT CLASSIC ANIMATED MOVIE FINDING NEMO (2003) TOOK $938 MILLION AT THE BOX OFFICE!

Finding Nemo!

Film-maker Andrew Stanton came up with the idea of making Clownfishes the stars of *Finding Nemo* when he saw a photo of two hiding in a sea anemone. He thought they looked very entertaining.

MONO SEBAE

This species is also known as an African Moony because of its home in the sea off the West African coast. It can grow up to 20.3 cm (8 in) long so it needs a pretty big tank! The Mono Sebae needs to be kept in brackish water, which is a cross between fresh and saltwater. It likes to eat seaweed and lettuce as well as special flake food.

FLUFFY FACT

Keeping tropical fish can be a very expensive hobby, with some species costing $388,000!

ZONE 5

Famous Friends

Movies, cartoons and video games are full of awesome pets...

the **lowdown...**

How To Train Your Dragon 2

This movie is set 5 years after the events of *How To Train Your Dragon* (2010). Team T-10's favorite movie pet, Toothless the Night Fury dragon, and his best buddy, Hiccup, have united the townsfolk of Berk island with dragons. It took over $46 million at the box office on its first weekend!

FLUFFY FACT

That adorable alien, E.T., was described in the first draft of the movie as actually being a plant! It's also not supposed to be considered a boy or a girl, or even an animal – just an alien.

TOP 10 Coolest Pet Movies

Who doesn't love a movie where an amazing pet is the star of the story? Here are Team T-10's fave live action and animated tales featuring pets.

	MOVIE	YEAR RELEASED
1	How To Train Your Dragon 2	2014
2	The Water Horse	2007
3	Frankenweenie	2012
4	Bolt	2008
5	E.T. the Extra-Terrestrial	1982
6	Babe	1995
7	The Cat Returns	2002
8	Scooby-Doo	2002
9	That Darn Cat!	1965
10	Lady & the Tramp	1955

AUTHOR DICK KING-SMITH WROTE THE BOOKS, "THE SHEEP PIG" (WHICH "BABE" WAS BASED ON) AND "THE WATER HORSE!"

BABE

Although this awesome piggy movie features lots of real animal actors, about 50 percent of the shots of *Babe* the pig were made with a mechanical puppet pig. It was created by Jim Henson's Creature Shop, which made *The Muppets*.

TOP 10 Most Successful Dog Movies

Humans' popular four-legged friends have been in hundreds of movies over the years, but these 10 are the ones that we loved the most.

	MOVIE	YEAR RELEASED	BOX OFFICE ($ WORLDWIDE)
1	101 Dalmations*	1996	320,689,294
2	Bolt	2008	309,979,994
3	Scooby-Doo	2002	275,650,703
4	Marley & Me	2008	242,717,113
5	101 Dalmations	1961	215,880,014
6	Cats & Dogs	2001	200,687,492
7	Beverly Hills Chihuahua	2008	149,281,606
8	Beethoven	1992	147,214,049
9	Hotel for Dogs	2009	117,000,198
10	Lady and the Tramp	1955	93,602,326

* Live action

BOX OFFICE

Each icon represents $25 million

Check out the ticket takings of these tales...

101 DALMATIONS*
$320,689,294

BOLT
$309,979,994

SCOOBY-DO
$275,650,703

FLUFFY FACT

Pop star and former Hannah Montana actor Miley Cyrus provides the voice for Penny, the owner of superstar stunt-dog Bolt!

Hotel for dogs

Almost 70 dogs were used to make *Hotel for Dogs* (2009) the hit movie it was. After filming was completed, 14 dog stars that needed homes were adopted by members of the movie crew. There was even a tie-in video game made for PC, and Nintendo Wii and DS systems.

HOW MANY OF THESE POOCH MOVIES HAVE YOU SEEN? SET UP A MOVIE NIGHT WITH YOUR FRIENDS!

the lowdown...

TWO FEMALES AND ONE MALE BOSTON TERRIER (CALLED DEEGAN) PLAYED THE GEORGIA ROLE IN HOTEL FOR DOGS! DEEGAN DID ALMOST ALL OF THE ACTION SCENES.

TOP 10 Highest-Paid Hollywood Animals

We've made all of these animal actors' salaries easy, so you can see the biggest non-human Hollywood earners.

	NAME	ANIMAL	MOST FAMOUS APPEARANCES	$ PER WEEK*
1	Bart	Bear	The Great Outdoors (movie)	139,928
2	Rin Tin Tin	German Shepherd	Appeared in 27 movies	66,973
3	Pal	Collie	Lassie (movie & TV)	37,070
4	Moose	Jack Russell Terrier	Frasier (TV)	14,656
5	Crystal	Capuchin Monkey	Night at the Museum (movie)	11,644
6	Teddy	Great Dane	Appeared in 18 movies	5,197
7	Terry	Cairn Terrier	The Wizard of Oz (movie)	2,008
8	Skippy	Wire Fox Terrier	The Thin Man (movie)	1,927
9	Higgins	Crossbreed dog	Benji (movie)	1,922
10	Trigger	Horse	Appeared in many westerns	929

*Adjusted for inflation

RIN TIN TIN

This German Shepherd had an adventurous life even before he became a superstar mutt. Born in September 1918, he was rescued from a First World War battle by US soldier Lee Duncan.

SIZE 'EM UP

Here's a quick visual comparison of the two stars' earnings.

RIN TIN TIN   PAL (LASSIE)

Pal (Lassie)

During Pal's 18-year-long life, he became the most famous Collie to ever play the world-famous, super-smart dog, Lassie. Pal made his debut in *Lassie Come Home* (1943) when he was 3 years old, and played Lassie in TV episodes, seven movies, promo events and more.

the lowdown...

TOP DOGS!
Lassie is also the star of over 50 books!

LET'S NOT FORGET KRYPTO THE SUPERDOG WHO CAME FROM SUPERMAN'S HOME PLANET OF KRYPTON!

A LITTLE GOLDEN BOOK
Lassie
and the Desie

FLUFFY FACT
Between 1947 and 1950, there was a hit radio show about Lassie, too.

TOP 10 Celebrity Pet Owners

Through social media, celebrities from the worlds of music, movies, TV and beyond love to share photos of their pet pals with us all. These 10 own fantastic dogs.

	CELEBRITY	PET	NAME
1	**Hugh Jackman**	**French Bulldog**	**Dali**
2	Amanda Seyfried	Australian Shepherd	Finn
3	Liv Tyler	Cavalier King Charles Spaniel	Neal
4	Peter Dinklage	Cross-breed	Kevin
5	Miley Cyrus	Rough Collie	Emu
6	Jon Hamm	Shepherd mix	Cora
7	Taylor Swift	Scottish Fold	Olivia Benson
8	Leo DiCaprio	Labrador Retriever	Spinee
9	Paris Hilton	Chihuahua	Malibu
10	Heidi Klum	Pomeranian	Buttercup

5 COOL DICAPRIO ANIMAL FACTS

1. He owns a giant tortoise.
2. In 2013, he donated $3 million to saving tigers in Nepal.
3. In 2014, his foundation pledged $7 million for ocean conservation projects.
4. He survived a shark attack.
5. In 2007, Nicolas Cage outbid him for a $267,000 dinosaur skull.

HOW'S THIS FOR WEIRD PETS? NICOLE KIDMAN RAISES ALPACAS AND VANILLA ICE HAS A KANGAROO!

WHO ARE YOUR FAVE CELEBS? DO YOU KNOW IF THEY HAVE ANY PETS THAT YOU LOVE TOO?

the **lowdown...**

Hugh Jackman

The man who plays lethal X-Man Wolverine clearly has a soft, dog-adoring side! Dali is a French Bulldog, a breed that is famous for being very loving and playful – the perfect pal to chill out with after long days filming action-packed, adamantium-clawed scenes!

FLUFFY FACT

Due to their bulky, muscular build, French Bulldogs have great difficulty keeping their body temperature stable. Therefore, they should not be left outside in the sun – owners need to make sure they're cool at all times.

TOP 10 Famous Cartoon Cats

The animation world has seen many, MANY famous animal characters become stars, but these are the most well-known kitties.

MY FAVE MOVIE STAR, BILL MURRAY, VOICED GARFIELD FOR THE TWO MOVIES RELEASED IN 2004 AND 2006.

the lowdown...

Garfield

Lasagna-loving Garfield was created and drawn by Jim Davis. After making his first appearance in a comic strip in 1978, he's starred in animated movies, TV specials, video games and fluffy toy merchandise galore.

	CHARACTER	APPEARED IN...
1	Garfield	Garfield
2	Tom	Tom & Jerry
3	Sylvester	Looney Tunes cartoons
4	Scratchy	The Itchy & Scratchy Show
5	Felix	Felix the Cat
6	Snowball II	The Simpsons
7	Mr Whiskers	Frankenweenie
8	Mitten	Bolt
9	Catbus	My Neighbor Totoro
10	Puss in Boots	Shrek films

SYLVESTER

Since his 1945 debut in the cartoon, the nemesis of cheeky yellow canary Tweety Pie has featured in over 100 cartoons!

FELIX THE CAT

Australian animator Pat Sullivan brought the famous Felix the Cat into the world with the cartoon *Felix Follies* all the way back in 1919! Since then, the character has starred in nearly 200 animated adventures.

FLUFFY FACT

Tom & Jerry first scrapped together in 1940! The duo have been through 10 different cartoon looks.

Top cats!

There are over 80 super-famous cats in the world of animation, which made this list very hard to do! Other kitties who didn't quite make the list include Jess from *Postman Pat*, Top Cat, and Dr Paul Hutchison from *Rocko's Modern Life*.

TOP 10 Biggest-Selling Digital Pets

Computer, console and key chain pets have been popular for decades, especially these 10...

	GAME/FRANCHISE	YEAR FIRST RELEASED	UNITS SOLD (MILLIONS)
1	Tamagotchi	1996	76
2	Nintendogs	2005	24.6
3	Petz	2005	15.07
4	The Sims: Pets	2009	11.41
5	MOPy Fish	1997	10
6	Nintendogs + Cats	2011	3.37
7	Spore	2008	2.99
8	Kinectimals	2010	1.82
9	Zoo Tycoon	2001	1.66
10	EyePet	2009	1.29

YOU CAN LOOK AFTER THE DINOSAURS IN THE 2003 GAME JURASSIC PARK: OPERATION GENESIS!

NINTENDOGS

Since its April 2005 release, the DS pet simulator has sold nearly 24 million copies! There were originally three types: Chihuahua & Friends, Dachshund & Friends, and Lab & Friends.

DID YOU KNOW?
"Tamagotchi" means "egg watch." It was invented by Japanese developers Akihiro Yokoi and Aki Maita.

WHICH CYBERPET WOULD YOU LIKE TO CARE FOR? WHY NOT TRY DESIGNING YOUR VERY OWN CREATURE!

the lowdown...

Tamagotchi

Way before the Nintendo DS appeared on the pet simulator scene, this egg-shaped key chain digital pet took the world by storm in 1996. But fear not, smartphones and tablets can now enjoy this, the original cyber-pet, with the 2013 version, Tamagotchi L.I.F.E. Tap and Hatch.

FLUFFY FACT
There have been nearly 50 different original Tamagotchis released, and that's not including the 18 video game versions that have appeared across Game Boy, DS, Wii and iPad.

TIME TO GET INTERACTIVE!

It's time to say goodbye to the cute and crazy pet pals we've met on our T-10 journey. See how well you've got to know them with this quick quiz...

Questions from... ZONE 1

1 Can you put these pets in order of how long they live? Start with the longest at number one..

 A
 B
 C

2 See if you know whether these facts about the White Lion cub are true or false.

A: The White Lion is an endangered animal.
TRUE FALSE

B: A cub costs over $485,206 to buy.
TRUE FALSE

C: A White Lion, Kalu, was left $77,633,298.
TRUE FALSE

3 Which of these is the biggest pet-owning country?
A: Brazil
B: China
C: USA

Questions from... ZONE 2

2 A The Irish Wolfhound is number one in which Top 10 list?

B Which dog breed is the fastest, reaching speeds of 69.2 km/h (43 mph)?

1 Can you name these three popular dog breeds just from seeing their silhouettes?

A **B** **C**

3 See if you can name this breed of domestic cat from what you can see in this picture.

Questions from... ZONE 3

1 Can you name two animals that appear in the Top 10 Smallest Rodent Pets list?

2 See if you can name the breed of these two super-cute pets.

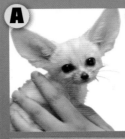
A

B

3 Here's a picture of the smallest rabbit breed in the world. Put a tick next to its name.

A: Netherland Dwarf ☐

B: Mini Plush Lop ☐

C: Himalayan ☐

Questions from... ZONE 4

1 Which exotic bird breed is so clever it's been called the Einstein of the bird world?

2 The star of *Finding Nemo* was based on which tropical fish?

3 Can you name this nocturnal pet from the jumbled image?

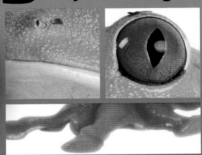

Questions from... ZONE 5

1 Can you name this lasagna-loving cat?

2 Which 2014 pet movie starred Toothless and Hiccup and took in over $46 million at the box office on its first weekend?

A: Bolt .... ☐

B: Scooby-Doo .... ☐

C: How To Train Your Dragon 2 ☐

D: Frankenweenie.......... ☐

3 At the peak of his career, how much did dog actor Rin Tin Tin earn in a week?

A: $139,927 ☐

B: $66,973 ☐

C: $37,070 ☐

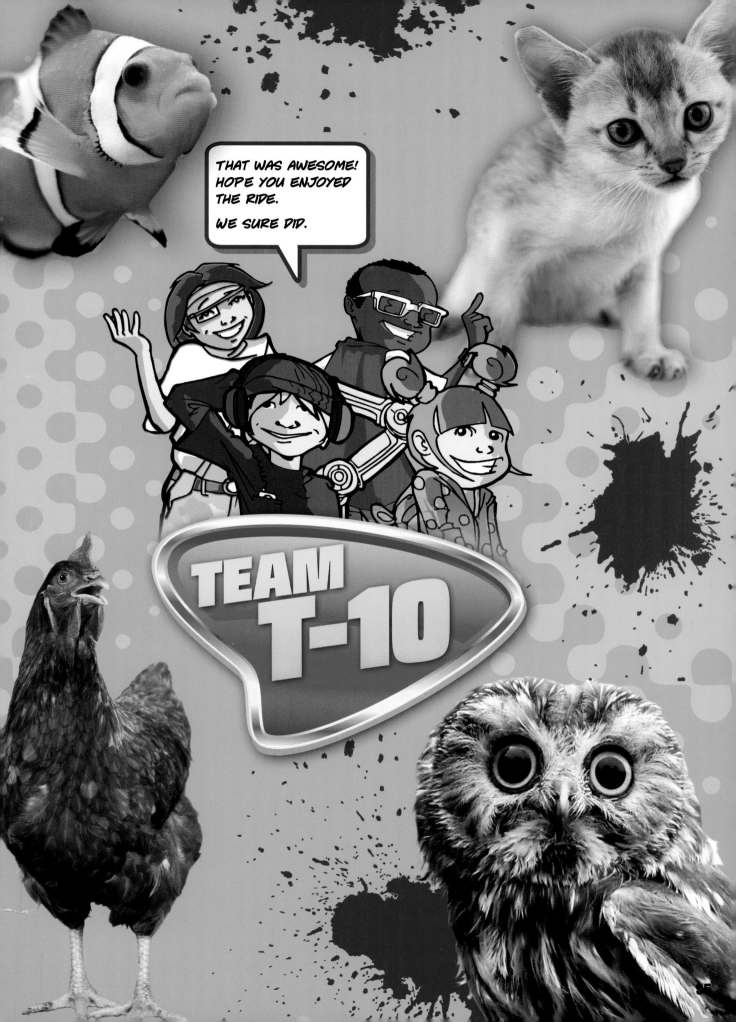

Also available:

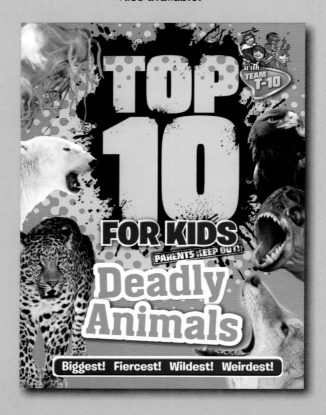

PICTURE CREDITS

All images supplied by © **Getty Images**

Except:

The Kobal Collection
P80: (BG) Dreamworks Animation / The Kobal Collection

. . . .

ACKNOWLEDGMENTS

Top 10 Parents Keep Out! Pets Produced by SHUBROOK BROS. CREATIVE

Writer & Researcher: Paul Terry

Illustrations: Huw J

Chief Sub-editor: Claire Bilsland

. . . .

Special thanks to...

Ian Turp & Marc Glanville at Getty Images

Box office information courtesy of The Internet Movie Database (http://www.imdb.com).
Used with permission.

. . . .